Last Days of the Dinosaurs

by Ruth Owen

Consultant:
Dougal Dixon, Paleontologist
Member of the Society of Vertebrate Paleontology
United Kingdom

BEARPORT PUBLISHING

New York, New York

Easy
567.9 owe

Credits

Cover, © Herschel Hoffmeyer/Shutterstock and © Warpaint/Shutterstock; 3, © Warpaint/Shutterstock; 4–5, © James Kuether; 6, © Allie Caulfield/Creative Commons; 7, © Andrej Antic/Shutterstock; 8, © solarseven/Shutterstock; 9, © Science Photo Library/Alamy; 10–11, © James Kuether; 12, © Mark Garlick/Science Photo Library; 13, © Science Photo Library/Alamy; 14–15, © James Kuether; 16–17, © D. Van Ravenswaay/Science Photo Library; 18–19, © Alex Mustard; 20, © Michael Rosskothen/Shutterstock; 21T, © Ryan M. Bolton/Shutterstock; 21BL, © Glass and Nature/Shutterstock; 21BR, © Stockphoto Mania/Shutterstock; 22T, © twiggins/Shutterstock; 22C, © solarseven/Shutterstock; 22B, © Michael Rosskothen/Shutterstock and © Panu Ruangjan/Shutterstock; 23T, © James Kuether; 23C, © Nadezda Murmakova/Shutterstock; 23B, © Romolo Tavani/Shutterstock.

Publisher: Kenn Goin
Senior Editor: Joyce Tavolacci
Creative Director: Spencer Brinker
Image Researcher: Ruth Owen Books

Library of Congress Cataloging-in-Publication Data

Names: Owen, Ruth, 1967– author.
Title: Last days of the dinosaurs / by Ruth Owen.
Description: New York, New York : Bearport Publishing, [2019] | Series: The dino-sphere | Includes bibliographical references and index.
Identifiers: LCCN 2018049813 (print) | LCCN 2018053175 (ebook) | ISBN 9781642802580 (Ebook) | ISBN 9781642801897 (library)
Subjects: LCSH: Dinosaurs—Extinction—Juvenile literature.
Classification: LCC QE861.6.E95 (ebook) | LCC QE861.6.E95 O94 2019 (print) | DDC 567.9—dc23
LC record available at https://lccn.loc.gov/2018049813

For more information, write to Bearport Publishing Company, Inc., 45 West 21st Street, Suite 3B, New York, New York 10010. Printed in the United States of America.

10 9 8 7 6 5 4 3 2 1

Contents

Lots of Dinosaurs

A *Tyrannosaurus rex* chases after a *Triceratops*.

The *T. rex* snaps its huge jaws.

Will it catch its meal?

Dinosaurs, like *T. rex* and *Triceratops*, lived on Earth millions of years ago.

Tyrannosaurus rex
(ti-ran-uh-SOR-uhss REKS)

Triceratops
(trye-SER-uh-tops)

Gone Forever

Today, there are no more living dinosaurs on Earth.

What happened to them?

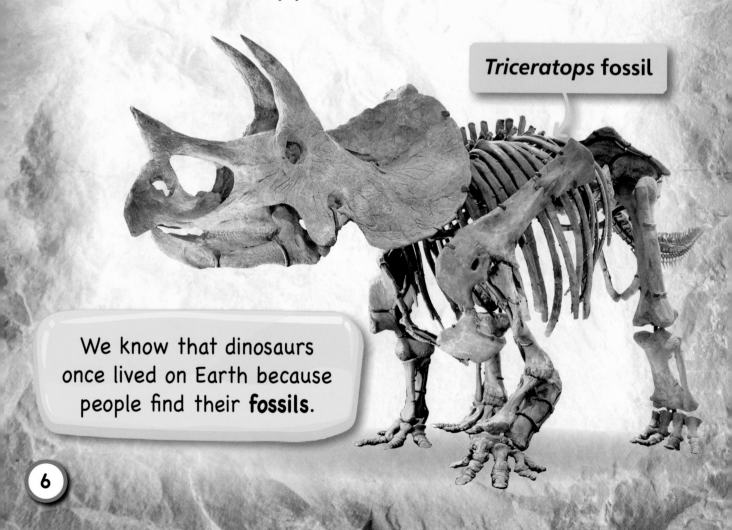

Triceratops fossil

We know that dinosaurs once lived on Earth because people find their **fossils**.

Scientists think they know the answer.

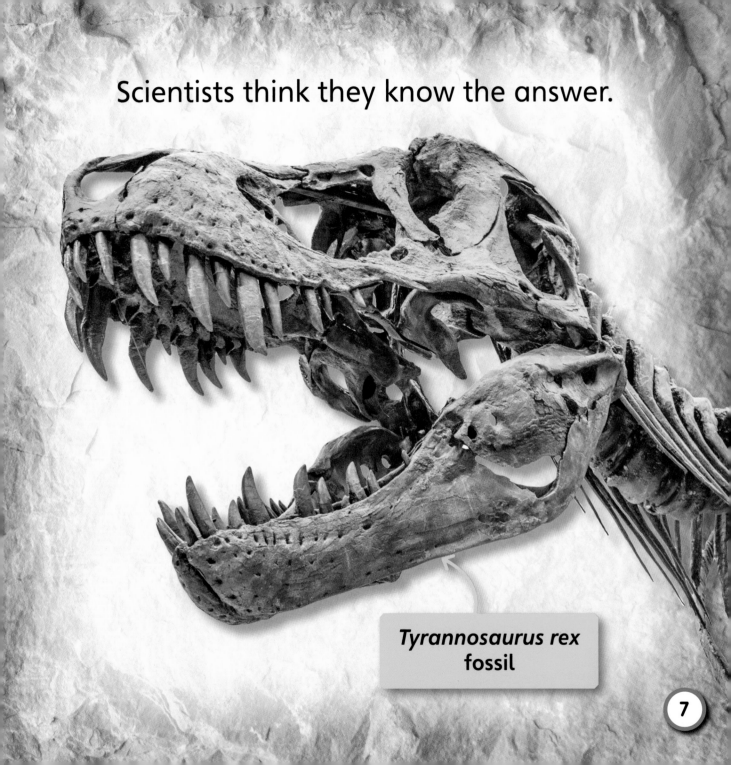

Tyrannosaurus rex
fossil

Asteroid Attack!

About 66 million years ago, a giant **asteroid** was flying through space.

It sped toward Earth.

asteroid

One day, the asteroid crashed into
Earth. *Boom!*

The asteroid was about
6 miles (10 km) wide!

Impact

When the asteroid struck Earth, it landed near the sea.

It made a giant hole in the ground.

It also created giant waves in the sea.

Many dinosaurs were killed.

The waves were higher than a 25-story building!

A Dark Land

Rocks, dust, and smoke filled the sky.

The Sun's light was blocked, and the land became dark.

Most of the plants died because there was no sunlight.

volcano

The asteroid shook the whole Earth. The land cracked open, causing **volcanoes** to erupt.

Doomed Dinosaurs

Soon, many more dinosaurs died.

The plant-eaters died because there was no food to eat.

Then, the meat-eating dinosaurs died. Why?

Eventually, there were no plant-eaters left to eat!

After the asteroid struck Earth, most kinds of dinosaurs became **extinct**.

A Giant Hole

How do we know an asteroid killed the dinosaurs?

Scientists found the remains of the giant hole.

It's about 90 miles (145 km) wide.

It's now under the sea, near Mexico.

The giant hole made by an asteroid is called a crater (KREY-ter.)

crater

Not Extinct!

Lots of different animals lived on Earth with the dinosaurs.

Some of them survived the **disaster**.

Crocodiles lived at the same time as *T. rex* and *Triceratops*.

Today, crocodiles still live on Earth.

crocodile

Scientists have found crocodile teeth and *T. rex* fossils together. This proves that they lived at the same time.

Dinosaurs All Around

Before the disaster, a group of dinosaurs related to *Velociraptors* **evolved**.

These dinosaurs became birds.

Some of the birds survived the asteroid strike.

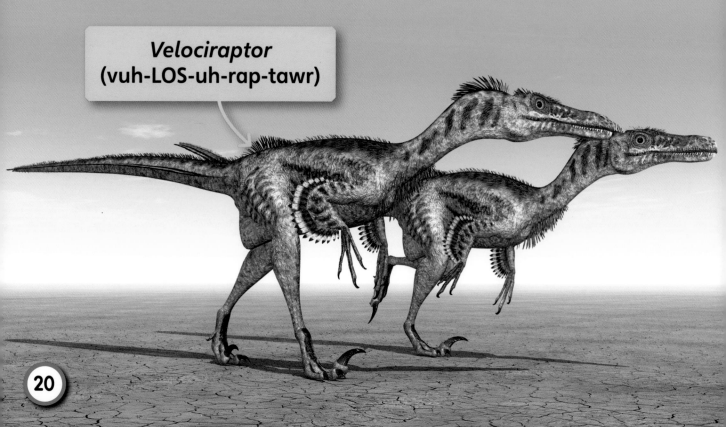

Velociraptor
(vuh-LOS-uh-rap-tawr)

Eventually, they became the birds of today!

All birds are related
to dinosaurs.

Glossary

asteroid (AS-teh-royd)
a large rock traveling
through space

disaster (duh-ZASS-tur)
something terrible that
happens suddenly and
causes lots of damage

evolved (ih-VOLVD)
changed gradually over
a long period of time

extinct (ek-STINGKT)
gone forever

fossils (FOSS-uhlz)
the rocky remains of
animals and plants
that lived millions
of years ago

volcanoes (vol-KAY-nohz)
openings in the Earth's
crust from which burning,
melted rock can erupt

Index

Read More

Bowman, Donna H. *Did Dinosaurs Eat People? And Other Questions Kids Have About Dinosaurs.* Minneapolis, MN: Picture Window Books (2011).

Woolley, Katie. *The Story of the Dinosaurs (Dinozone).* New York: Rosen (2017).

Learn More Online

To learn more about dinosaurs, visit
www.bearportpublishing.com/dinosphere

About the Author

Ruth Owen has been developing and writing children's books for more than ten years. She first discovered dinosaurs when she was four years old—and loves them as much today as she did then!